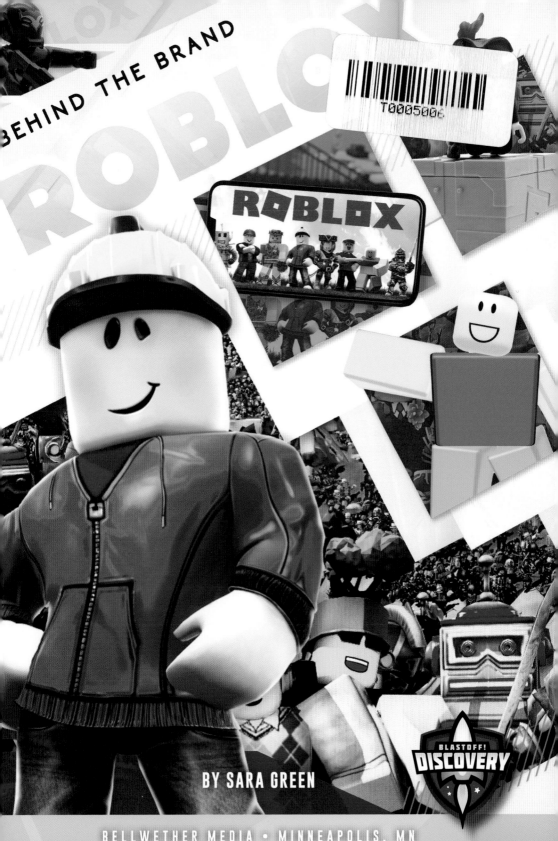

BEHIND THE BRAND

ROBLOX

T000500ᗺ

BY SARA GREEN

BLASTOFF! DISCOVERY

BELLWETHER MEDIA • MINNEAPOLIS, MN

Blastoff! Discovery launches a new mission: reading to learn. Filled with facts and features, each book offers you an exciting new world to explore!

BLASTOFF! UNIVERSE

BLASTOFF! Beginners — GRADE K

BLASTOFF! READERS — GRADES 1-3

BLASTOFF! DISCOVERY — GRADE 4

This edition first published in 2024 by Bellwether Media, Inc.

Library of Congress Cataloging-in-Publication Data

Names: Green, Sara, 1964- author.
Title: Roblox / By Sara Green.
Description: Minneapolis, MN : Bellwether Media, Inc., 2024. | Series:
    Blastoff! Discovery: Behind the brand | Includes bibliographical
    references and index. | Audience: Ages 7-13 | Audience: Grades 3-8 |
    Summary: "Engaging images accompany information about Roblox. The
    combination of high-interest subject matter and narrative text is
    intended for students in grades 3 through 8"–Provided by publisher.
Identifiers: LCCN 2023007737 (print) | LCCN 2023007738 (ebook) |
    ISBN 9798886874488 (library binding) | ISBN 9798886875409 (paperback) |
    ISBN 9798886876369 (ebook)
Subjects: LCSH: Roblox (Computing platform)–Juvenile literature.
Classification: LCC GV1469.35.R594 G72 2024 (print) | LCC GV1469.35.R594
    (ebook) | DDC 794.8/1513–dc23/eng/20230222
LC record available at https://lccn.loc.gov/2023007737
LC ebook record available at https://lccn.loc.gov/2023007738

Editor: Betsy Rathburn   Designer: Andrea Schneider

Printed in the United States of America, North Mankato, MN.

TABLE OF
CONTENTS

A ROBLOX ADVENTURE!

After finishing his homework, a boy logs in to Roblox to play *Adopt Me!* This **role-playing game** is a popular Roblox experience!

The boy moves his **avatar** through the **virtual** world. Other avatars chat and walk with their pets along the busy streets. The boy's avatar stops at the Nursery. He is saving up to buy a Royal Egg. One day, he may hatch a rare alicorn! Next, the boy visits his virtual home. He feeds his Starter Egg a sandwich. Soon, it will hatch into a cat. Roblox is full of fun experiences!

ADOPT ME!
VIRTUAL WORLD

Starter Egg
Unhatched

STARTER EGG

LAUNCHING ROBLOX

ROBLOX HEADQUARTERS
SAN MATEO, CALIFORNIA

Roblox is an online game **platform** made by the Roblox **Corporation**. The company's **headquarters** is in San Mateo, California. Roblox can be played for free on computers, **consoles**, and mobile devices. More than 60 million people worldwide play Roblox every day!

Roblox brings people together in the **metaverse**. There, they can meet, explore, and learn through play. Roblox offers millions of games, known as experiences. Players can build, explore, fight, and chat with friends. The possibilities are endless on Roblox!

BIG BUCKS

The Roblox Corporation was worth more than $20 billion in 2023!

ROBLOX HEADQUARTERS

SAN MATEO, CALIFORNIA

In 1989, a computer scientist named David Baszucki started a company called Knowledge Revolution. Its purpose was to teach students about physics. David and his employee Erik Cassel created computer programs about physics. Students used the programs to make buildings fall and cars crash. The programs were a hit!

DAVID BASZUCKI

BORN
January 20, 1963, in Canada

ROLE
Co-founder and leader of the Roblox Corporation

ACCOMPLISHMENTS
Led the growth of Roblox to become one of the most successful online game platforms of all time

David sold Knowledge Revolution in 1998. But he wanted to continue making physics fun for students. In 2004, David teamed up with Erik to create a new company called DynaBlocks. The name was soon changed to Roblox. David and Erik thought this name was easier to remember.

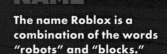

A CREATIVE NAME

The name Roblox is a combination of the words "robots" and "blocks."

SUNSET PLAIN

Roblox was released on September 1, 2006. Most early experiences, such as *Rocket Arena* and *Chaos Canyon*, were **developed** by Roblox. Some users began developing their own games, too. An early game called *Sunset Plain* is still popular with fans. By the end of 2006, Roblox had around 11,000 users.

More features were added to Roblox in 2007. Users could **customize** their avatars and earn virtual money called Roblox Points. A safe chat feature also came out. David and Erik then began to **advertise** on YouTube. The number of Roblox users soared!

EARLY ROBLOX GAMES

	TYPE	YEAR CREATED	STILL AVAILABLE?
ROCKET ARENA	FIGHTING	2006	NO
SUNSET PLAIN	FIGHTING	2006	YES
BASE WARS	FIRST-PERSON SHOOTER	2007	YES
CHAOS CANYON	FIGHTING	2007	NO
CROSSROADS	FIGHTING	2007	YES

In 2007, Roblox ended Roblox Points. It introduced two new forms of virtual money called Tickets and Robux. Players earned Tickets, or Tix, each time they logged onto Roblox. Tix ended in 2016, but Robux is still used today.

A FUN JOB!

More than 2,200 Roblox developers earned $10,000 or more in 2021!

ROBLOX DEVELOPERS

Flowy Supermodel hair
◉ 75

AVATAR SHOP

Spy Cap

Joyful Smile
◉ 20

Candy Apple Hair
◉ 80

Shiny Teeth
◉ 35

Spring Green Bo
◉ 50

Players can earn Robux or buy Robux with real money. They use Robux to buy items for avatars and games. Game developers over the age of 13 can also earn Robux. Many do this by selling games or items for avatars. They use the Developer Exchange Program to turn Robux into real money.

Roblox continued to gain fans. By 2012, Roblox had more than 20 million users! By the mid-2010s, Roblox was available on Xbox, computers, and mobile devices. Roblox launched Roblox VR on Oculus Rift in 2016. Players use **virtual reality** headsets to step inside games!

By the end of 2019, more than 100 million people played Roblox each month. Most were kids under the age of 16. The COVID-19 **pandemic** led to even greater numbers. Many kids stayed indoors. They played Roblox games and attended virtual birthday parties, concerts, and other events. The number of monthly users soared to more than 200 million in 2021!

A POPULAR HOBBY

Over half of kids under age 16 living in the United States played Roblox in 2020!

VIRTUAL BIRTHDAY PARTY

BUILDING MORE FUN

BROOKHAVEN RP

Today, Roblox continues to delight users around the world. It offers more than 30 million experiences. *Adopt Me!* is a popular multiplayer game. Total visits number more than 30 billion! Players take care of animals, build homes, and chat with friends. They can make trades and buy eggs that hatch pets. The pets include dolphins, elephants, and dragons!

Brookhaven RP is a popular role-playing game with more than 25 billion visits. Users enter the town of Brookhaven. There, they can hang out with friends, drive fast cars, and decorate houses. Brookhaven has many secret spots hidden around town. Players find them as they explore!

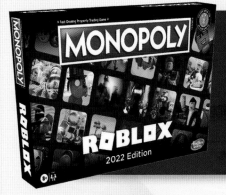

OFF-SCREEN PLAY

A toy company called Hasbro introduced Roblox into some of its products. Some Nerf blasters are based on Roblox experiences. There is even a Roblox edition of *Monopoly!*

WORK AT A
PIZZA PLACE

MEGA EASY OBBY

Other experiences offer even more fun. Obstacle courses, or obbies, are fun challenges. Users tackle obstacles including mazes and lava jumps to reach the end of the course. *Mega Easy Obby* is a popular obstacle course game. Fighting games such as *Ninja Legends 2* are loaded with action. Players test their skills as they battle enemies!

Other experiences let users try new things! In *Strongman Simulator*, players use their avatars to move heavy things. They try to be the strongest player! In *Work at a Pizza Place*, users cook, box, and deliver pizzas. Roblox experiences are endless!

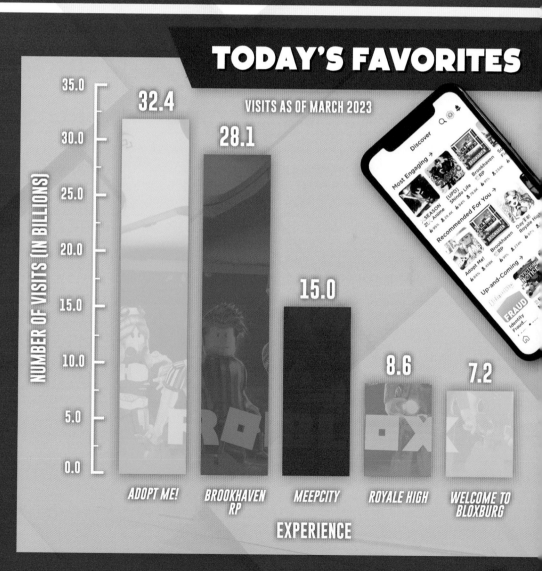

TODAY'S FAVORITES

VISITS AS OF MARCH 2023

NUMBER OF VISITS (IN BILLIONS)

Experience	Visits (billions)
ADOPT ME!	32.4
BROOKHAVEN RP	28.1
MEEPCITY	15.0
ROYALE HIGH	8.6
WELCOME TO BLOXBURG	7.2

EXPERIENCE

Real-life items and places can also be found in the Roblox metaverse. Players can collect fancy clothes in *Gucci Town* or make a meal in *Chipotle Burrito Builder*. In *NIKELAND*, they can play soccer, try on gear, and jump on trampolines. *Vans World* has skate parks where users can show off their moves!

GUCCI TOWN

NIKELAND

VIRTUAL LIL NAS X CONCERT

VANS WORLD

In 2020, Lil Nas X became the first musician to perform virtual concerts in the Roblox metaverse. His four concerts drew 33 million views! Since then, Roblox has hosted many other concerts and music events. Games and prizes are often part of the fun!

IMPROVED GRAPHICS

LAYERED CLOTHING
AND ACCESSORIES

The Roblox metaverse continues to improve. Better **graphics** make materials such as sand and wood look more real. Avatars can smile, wink, and scrunch their foreheads. Their body shapes can be customized with the click of a button. Fashion choices include layered clothing and many different **accessories**!

Roblox is also making it easier for people to connect with each other in the metaverse. Users who are age 13 and older can use voice chat to talk to friends.

POPULAR AVATAR ITEMS

ITEM	NUMBER OF FAVORITES	COST IN ROBUX
BEAR FACE MASK	MORE THAN 2 MILLION	100
ROBLOX BASEBALL CAP	MORE THAN 791,000	FREE
BANANA SUIT	MORE THAN 308,000	100
FLAMINGO FLOATY	MORE THAN 216,000	50

Roblox users do not only play games and chat. Many also make their own experiences! Roblox lets users build all types of games. Coding skills are not needed to create simple games. To build advanced games, users learn a coding language called Lua. Lua is easy to learn. Even beginners can start developing games after a few lessons!

Developers can create avatar accessories, too. They can make hats, shirts, masks, and more. Other users can buy these items. Developers can earn Robux when others buy their items. Roblox is a fun way to play, create, and earn!

ROBLOX DEVELOPERS

LUA CODING LANGUAGE

ROBLOX TIMELINE

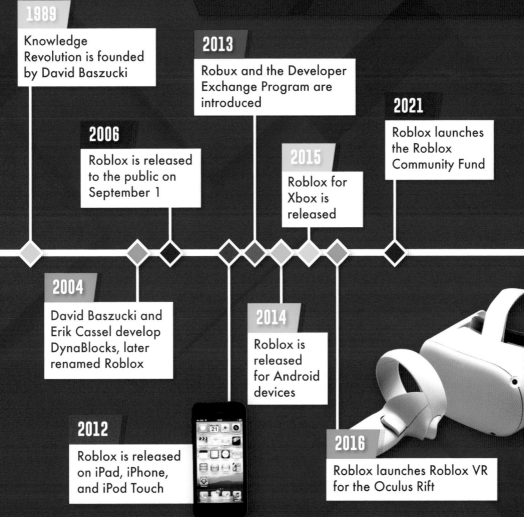

1989
Knowledge Revolution is founded by David Baszucki

2013
Robux and the Developer Exchange Program are introduced

2021
Roblox launches the Roblox Community Fund

2006
Roblox is released to the public on September 1

2015
Roblox for Xbox is released

2004
David Baszucki and Erik Cassel develop DynaBlocks, later renamed Roblox

2014
Roblox is released for Android devices

2012
Roblox is released on iPad, iPhone, and iPod Touch

2016
Roblox launches Roblox VR for the Oculus Rift

BEYOND ROBLOX

Roblox is not the only place where Lua is used. The popular game *Angry Birds* is mostly written in Lua!

HELPING OUT

MUSEUM OF SCIENCE MARS PROJECT

Roblox supports programs that help kids learn. In 2020, a special event helped raise $100,000 to support Code.org and the Make-A-Wish **Foundation**.

GAME FUND

The Game Fund was launched in 2021. It pays a small group of developers to create new experiences! A Game Fund experience called *Winds of Fortune* came out in 2022!

In 2021, the Roblox Corporation launched the Roblox Community Fund, or RCF. It gives money to projects that help kids learn. The Museum of Science in Boston used RCF money to help kids plan a mission to Mars. Roblox has also teamed up with Project Lead the Way. Together, they will help students explore game development from inside the Roblox metaverse!

GIVING BACK

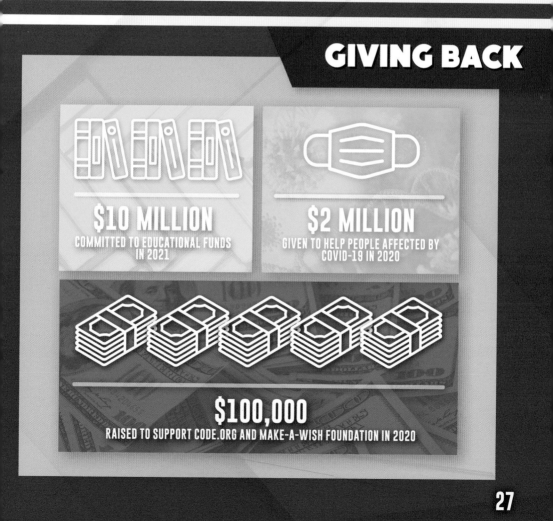

$10 MILLION
COMMITTED TO EDUCATIONAL FUNDS IN 2021

$2 MILLION
GIVEN TO HELP PEOPLE AFFECTED BY COVID-19 IN 2020

$100,000
RAISED TO SUPPORT CODE.ORG AND MAKE-A-WISH FOUNDATION IN 2020

CELEBRATING ROBLOX

ROBLOX DEVELOPER CONFERENCE

There are many ways to enjoy Roblox. Each year, Roblox hosts an event called the Roblox Developer **Conference**, or RDC. Only the top Roblox developers are invited to attend in person. Others can stream the event.

The RDC is packed with activities. Developers share ideas and get updates about Roblox. The Game Jam is a highlight. Teams of developers race to create a new Roblox game! An awards ceremony ends the RDC. Awards are given to top games and developers in categories such as Best New Experience and Best Use of Avatar Fashion. Roblox sparks creativity in endless ways!

2022 ROBLOX AWARD WINNERS

BEST NEW EXPERIENCE

Deepwoken by Vows by the Sea

BEST USE OF AVATAR FASHION

Mermaid Life by FullflowerGames

VIDEO STAR OF THE YEAR

Flamingo

BEST INTERNATIONAL HIT

Welcome to Bloxburg by Coeptus

PEOPLE'S CHOICE

BedWars by Easy.gg

GLOSSARY

accessories—items added to something else to make it more useful or attractive

advertise—to announce or promote something to get people to buy or use it

avatar—a figure representing a certain person in a video game

conference—a large meeting of people to talk about shared work or interests

consoles—electronic devices for playing video games

corporation—a large company

customize—to make or change something to fit a user's needs

developed—created

foundation—an organization that gives money to people or groups in need

graphics—art such as illustrations or designs

headquarters—a company's main office

metaverse—a system of linked virtual worlds where users communicate with each other as avatars

pandemic—an outbreak of a disease over a whole country or the world

platform—an app or other software on which people can play video games

role-playing game—a game in which players take on roles of characters to complete the game

virtual—something created by computer technology that appears to be real but does not exist in the physical world

virtual reality—related to computer technology that makes users feel like they are somewhere that does not really exist

TO LEARN MORE

AT THE LIBRARY

Duling, Kaitlyn. *Level Up: Secrets of the Games We Love*. Vero Beach, Fla.: Rourke Educational Media, 2021.

Green, Sara. *Minecraft*. Minneapolis, Minn.: Bellwether Media, 2023.

Gregory, Josh. *Games and Genres in Roblox*. Ann Arbor, Mich.: Cherry Lake Publishing, 2021.

ON THE WEB

FACTSURFER

Factsurfer.com gives you a safe, fun way to find more information.

1. Go to www.factsurfer.com.

2. Enter "Roblox" into the search box and click Q.

3. Select your book cover to see a list of related content.

INDEX

The images in this book are reproduced through the courtesy of: Shaf Moment, front cover (avatar); Diego Thomazini, front cover (smartphone); Mariayunira, front cover (character); Wirestock, Inc./ Alamy, front cover (pirate); Wirestock Creators, front cover (LEGO), pp. 4-5; miglagoa, front cover (game background); Andrea Schneider, pp. 2-3 (avatar), 18 (*Work at a Pizza Place*); PremiumBeat, p. 3; Betsy Rathburn, pp. 5 (Starter Egg, *Adopt Me!* virtual world), 10 (chat feature, *Sunset Plain*), 13 (avatar shop), 15 (virtual birthday party), 16-17 (*Brookhaven RP*), 18 (*Mega Easy Obby*), 20 (*Gucci Town, NIKELAND*), 22 (improved graphics, layered clothing), 23 (all), 26 (Museum of Science Mars project); Coolcaesar/ Wikipedia, p. 6 (headquarters); goir, p. 7 (money); digidreamgrafix, p. 7 (San Mateo, California); REUTERS/ Alamy, p. 8 (David Baszucki); Sergey Elagin, p. 9 (smartphone); Wikipedia, p. 9 (DynaBlocks logo); stickpng, p. 9 (robot); Ian Tuttle/ Getty Images, pp. 12 (developers), 13 (Roblox developers), 24 (Roblox developers), 29 (Roblox Developer Conference, award winners); seventyfour, p. 12 (gamer); wachiwit, p. 14; cmspic, p. 15 (child); kcdealsandsteals, p. 17 (*Monopoly*); Bloomberg/ Getty Images, p. 19 (smartphone); AlexX, p. 24 (Lua coding language); Thomas Dutour, p. 25 (2012); Boumenjapet, p. 25 (2016); Mano Kors, p. 25 (*Angry Birds*); PNGAA, p. 31.